While every precaution has been taken in the preparation of this book, the publisher assumes no responsibility for errors or omissions, or for damages resulting from the use of the information contained herein.

BREAKING CHAINS: A MOTHER'S JOURNEY TO HEALING AND REDEMPTION

First edition. March 7, 2024.

Copyright © 2024 Nathlee R. Grant.

ISBN: 979-8224305872

Written by Nathlee R. Grant.

Table of Contents

THE AWAKENING...1

THE EPIPHANY 3

THE BEAST 6

THE CONQUEST...8

EXPERIENCING AND EXPRESSING HEALING GRACE. 10

FROM VICTIM TO VICTOR.. 13

THE NEW LIFE 16

APPLICATION 19

1. Create a safe environment!.. 24

2. Facilitate mutual respect 28

3. Spending quality time 32

4. Developing consistency 35

5. Fostering effective communication.................................... 38

6. Setting ground rules... 41

ADDITIONAL RESOURCES 44

Breaking Chains: A Mother's Journey to Healing and Redemption

Discovering the Healing Power of Love, Redemption and Spiritual Transformation

By: Nathlee R. Grant
Editor: Zowayne Williams

THE DISCOVERY....

"**B**ut for you who revere my name, the sun of righteousness will rise with *healing* in its rays...."

-Malachi 2:4

〈 〉

Love is very patient and kind, never jealous or envious, never boastful or proud, never haughty or selfish or rude. Love does not demand its own way. It is not irritable or touchy. It does not hold grudges and will hardly even notice when others do it wrong. It is never glad about injustice but rejoices whenever truth wins out. If you love someone, you will be loyal to him no matter what the cost. You will always believe in him, always expect the best of him, and always stand your ground in defending him."

-1 Corinthians 13: 4-7

"And that is what some of you were. But you were washed, you were sanctified, you were justified in the name of the Lord Jesus Christ and by the Spirit of our God."

-1 Corinthians 6:11

PREFACE

Emotional abuse is like a destructive hurricane ripping through a city, leaving devastation in its wake. Just as a city needs proper resources to rebuild after such a catastrophe, so too does a person affected by emotional abuse require the right tools for repair. Without them, they risk being trapped in a cycle of destruction, repeatedly experiencing the same pain and turmoil.

Imagine facing each new season with the looming threat of another hurricane, knowing that without proper rebuilding resources, you'll end up right back where you started when the storm inevitably hits again! This is the reality for those who haven't sought the necessary healing and restoration from emotional abuse.

If left unrepaired, the damage from emotional abuse can perpetuate through generations, like a destructive legacy passed down from parent to child. Just as disobedience to God had far-reaching consequences for biblical figures, our unresolved emotional wounds can have a lasting impact on our families and future generations.

Recognizing our own state of disrepair is crucial. In moments of anger or disappointment, our thoughts and words can either perpetuate destruction or sow seeds of healing and growth. Instead of allowing our emotions to dictate harmful reactions towards our children, we can choose to channel that energy into prayer. Praying for, with, and over our children fosters an environment of love and blessing, setting them on a path towards a brighter future.

By acknowledging our need for renewal and seeking the right resources for repair, we have the power to change the narrative for ourselves and future generations. It's through this spiritual authority of parenthood that we can break the cycle of destruction and pass on a legacy of healing and hope.

ACKNOWLEGEMENT

The process of crafting this book spanned years of personal healing, writing, and accumulated experience. Along this transformative journey, I've been blessed with the presence of significant individuals who have supported me in my healing process. Some of them I've never met, while others have become cherished friends and mentors. I owe a debt of gratitude to Ms. Faith Gordon and the Rev. Dr. Stephen Jennings whose wisdom and guidance have deeply influenced me. Distilling all that I've learned and felt into written words was a challenging and cathartic endeavor, made possible through the dedicated efforts of my primary editor and son, Zowayne Williams.

This work was further enriched by the invaluable feedback I received from close friends who possess exceptional command of the English language and superior writing skills, namely Ms. Caryline Whyte and Mrs. Eunice Lorde-Thomas. Yet, beyond mere grammatical refinement, I found reassurance in the content from my dear sister, Ms. Shelley Ann Simpson, longstanding friends Ms. Nicole Dickson and Ms. Carolyn Miller; and, my daughter, Ms. Yonique Bennett.

Ultimately, I attribute the fruition of this book to the grace of God, who not only facilitated the presence of these remarkable individuals in my life but also guided me through this arduous and transformative journey. It is with deep reverence and affection that I dedicate this book to the memory of my grandmother, the late Esther Cecelia Brown.

INTRODUCTION

Convinced of her daughter's forthcoming failure, a mother unconsciously replicated a familiar pattern of negative expressions in rage and anger. Repeatedly, she pronounced failure over her daughter's life, with harsh words such as, "You won't amount to anything, you are nothing but a time waster, you are an idiot." Yet, in the midst of this overwhelming frustration and anger, a transformative moment unfolded. A gentle yet powerful voice cut through the chaos, urging her to reconsider her approach to motherhood.

This pivotal message laden with the potential to confront and break the cycle of past mothering, marked the beginning of a profound transformation. This revelation forced her into an uncomfortable confrontation with her methods and compelled her to contemplate a paradigm shift.

She had no idea of the impact of a simple yet profound act. An act which included spending time with her daughter. This was initially dismissed, with her rationale echoing the neglect she had experienced in her own upbringing. It was further resisted by a deep-seated pride and a sense of entitlement to familiar behaviours. So it was that rationale and pride would sacrifice her daughter's success, stubbornly refusing to change the trajectory of her future. Overcoming this resistance became an arduous journey, requiring profound introspection and an honest confrontation with painful memories. Nevertheless, it was acted on, and life as mother and daughter knew it began to change.

Empathizing with the frustrations that mothers face, this reflection serves as a testament that releasing pent-up frustrations on children is never a solution. It only perpetuates a cycle of debris. The struggles faced by children are often mirrored in the experiences of their mothers. The call is clear – let's break free from any destructive pattern that binds us today and become the mothers our children need, for we want to guide them toward a successful future, even where this means to *mother differently*.

THE AWAKENING

It was my earlier commitment to follow Jesus that laid the foundation for the profound encounter to come. Bible verses about God's plans and purpose started to resonate with me, stirring a sense of belonging and purpose. This newfound understanding, however, extended beyond a personal revelation to a recognition of God's unique plans for His children, including my daughter.

Acknowledging the need for repair, I sought God's guidance. During this period there was evidence that the vessel that once navigated motherhood with flaws and faults was undergoing a transformation. I became conscious of the authoritative position I had taken in my children's lives. I, therefore, made deliberate efforts to speak words that would build them up rather than tear them down. Nonetheless, while repair is ongoing, the crucial shift lies in the acknowledgment of God's ownership of my children and my ability to call upon Him when uncertainty arises.

This journey, though challenging, stands as evidence to the possibility of change, growth, and the power of embracing a different motherhood. It serves as a beacon of hope for mothers seeking to redefine their roles and nurture their children according to a purposeful and loving plan. The ongoing transformation is a dynamic process, illustrating the potential for continuous growth and improvement in the realm of motherhood.

I had started paying attention to my behaviours and responses, forging connections with childhood experiences. This self-reflection marked the genesis of a transformative journey. This newfound self-awareness led me to a contemplative exploration of those around me; a quest to understand the shared experiences among siblings, relatives, neighbours, friends, co-workers, and even my adult children. It became evident that their adult responses mirrored my own. Behaviours that once seemed normative and righteous for years were now under the scrutiny of my newfound awareness. My investigations revealed an unsettling truth. With each revelation came a cascade of questions. The realization that our collective tapestry bore the imprints of shared upbringing ignited in me a sense of concern. Were we unknowingly perpetuating a cycle that needed breaking? This question propelled me into a quest for answers.

Why did certain reactions feel ingrained and how were they shaping my choices and relationships?

The answer was unsettling — I had been living in the shadows of *emotional abuse* my entire life. Emotional abuse refers to patterns of behaviour that harm an individual's emotional well-being and self-worth. It can include manipulation, intimidation, humiliation, gaslighting, and other tactics aimed at controlling or demeaning the victim. It's a serious form of abuse that can have long-lasting effects on a person's mental health and self-esteem. It cast its shadow on every decision I made, influencing my approach to parenting, finances, relationships, career choices, and various other aspects of my life. Subsequently, I unconsciously perpetuated and inflicted upon others this very same abuse.

Hurting people hurt; it's a cycle that infiltrates generations. An emotionally unwell individual, unknowingly, drains emotions from others, continuing the pattern of abuse. This toxic legacy doesn't confine itself to the home but penetrates every aspect of life, including professional relationships and friendships. The unseen beast of emotional abuse sinks its teeth into every facet of an individual's existence.

THE EPIPHANY

My awakening to the cycle of hurt happened in an unexpected moment. It was 2014, close to my daughter's final exams, and I was convinced she was on a path to failure. In a fit of rage, I spoke words of fear and despair over her, echoing the destructive patterns I inherited from my own upbringing. But in that moment of darkness, a gentle voice cut through, delivering a message that would alter the trajectory of generations, "If you don't want your daughter to repeat your academic struggles, you must stop mothering her the way your mother did you."

Ironically, the child who once cried foul play grows into a parent who mirrors the actions of their predecessor, i.e. convinced of their own rightness while deeming their child wrong. This revelation hit me hard. I realized I had been mirroring my mother's parenting style without even realizing it. The path to change wasn't easy, but it was necessary. I had to acknowledge the root of my reactions, embracing this painful process to eventually find healing through forgiveness.

Upon introspection, many may discover that the root cause of their distress lies in the perceived threat to their authority or power, or perhaps the fear of looking or feeling inadequate. Recognizing one's own value and worth can be transformative, fostering confidence and diminishing a sense of threat. This newfound clarity enables one to attack an issue and not a person, knowing for certain that an issue is an issue and a person a person thereby distinguishing the two.

For the longest time I was unable to do this. My heart harboured the weight of negativity, particularly towards my mother. As I relentlessly pursued the negatives, I failed to acknowledge the positive aspects of my mother's character. It was a darkness fueled by my selective focus on her flaws, rendering me blind to the positives she brought to my life as she performed countless acts of kindness and love that I had overlooked. Consumed by bitterness and hatred, I fixated on the negative actions and words that manifested from her, overshadowing even moments of joy. I found it impossible to recognize the love that existed and was ignorant that it sought expression beneath the surface.

I failed to see the hopelessness in my mother's eyes as she coped with the loss of her dreams, shattered by her own naivety. The shock of realizing that fairy tales were mere illusions, and that the struggles of living had altered her life in ways she never anticipated. Her fights were an effort to maintain a semblance of safety and to protect me from the perceived terrors that life might bring. My mother in her own way mothered me the best way she knew. The pain she carried and passed on made it difficult for me to interpret her cries as warnings of potential danger, instead I saw them as dismissive declarations of my unworthiness. The negative voice of her lips drowned out the voice of her heart, leaving me unable to comprehend the love that existed behind the slaps and rebukes.

In such situations, my heart became hardened to love, the essence of life, and was thus rendered almost impenetrable. The belief that my mother didn't love me was not only a reflection of my marred perception, but also a manifestation of my own struggle with self-love. Consequently, I spent a significant portion of my life living defensively, attempting to shield myself from perceived threats.

In the pursuit of effective parenting, a reflective journey unfolded as I grappled with the scriptural directive, "Parents do not provoke your children to wrath." Unbeknownst to me, my actions were inadvertently provoking anger in my children. Initially, I misinterpreted the biblical injunction, equating "provoke" with mere teasing. Little did I realize that my rigid parenting methods, rooted in societal expectations, were provocations causing emotional harm. The harsh judgments, cursing, and name-calling were shaping a toxic environment for my children.

A wake-up call came when I recognized the intelligence and brilliance of my children and could acknowledge my failure in nurturing these qualities. I recognised that I magnified weaknesses and overlooked strengths - a disaster to their self-esteem. This forced me to question the kind of mother I was, driven by societal standards, rather than having a genuine concern for my children's well-being. I found that I struggled to see the good in what I had. Ungratefulness, a silent sin, was identified as a root cause of my actions. The refusal to appreciate what I had led to an insatiable hunger for external validations. From relationships to material possessions, my pursuit of fulfilment remained unquenched.

THE BEAST

Emotional abuse, the silent assailant, emerged as the culprit shaping my worldview. Its insidious influence seeped into every crevice of my existence, leaving an indelible mark on my perceptions and decisions. Left unidentified and untreated, it destructively passes through generations, robbing the beauty of parent-child relationships and eroding persons of self- esteem and confidence. The weight of hopelessness then settles in, casting a dark cloud over life's potential. Without intervention, it perpetuates, echoing through generations like an unbroken chain of despair.

Now that I knew that I was bound by emotional abuse, I wanted freedom but attempting to break its grip proved challenging. Even when I summoned the courage to try, success felt elusive. Deep down, a distorted self- perception festered, convincing me that success was a realm reserved for others, never close enough for me to touch. The shadows of unworthiness clung stubbornly, making every attempt at success an uphill battle. The journey to break free from these shadows became a formidable task, demanding resilience, and self-discovery. The emotional abuse I endured left me emotionally unwell, attributing my unhappiness and failures to external factors. Blame became my shield, a defense mechanism against the lurking threats of failure, mistrust, and fear. Emotional unwellness became the lens through which I viewed the world.

The privilege to express my voice was a casualty of this abuse, a voice that fear compelled me to silence. I thus found solace in the crowd, one that echoed facets of my own voice. Silencing my voice became a survival mechanism. Fear of judgment and criticism stifled my authentic expression and pushed me into the safety of conformity.

The life of emotional abuse unfolded as a web of lies and death, woven by the inability to decipher my feelings. Faced with the daunting task of acknowledging the pain, I often sought refuge in denial. The lies of emotional abuse had entrenched my psyche. Denial became a comforting veil, shielding me from the harsh realities of my emotional wounds. Denial, however, is a lie itself — a lie that whispers we have no value and no worth. It denies us the gift of self-confidence and assurance, branding us with the mark of the beast, that is, in this case, emotional abuse. Removing this brand and freeing oneself requires dismantling the lies embedded in our beliefs. It demands a courageous confrontation with the distorted narratives that have dictated our sense of self.

As I reflect on my struggles, I recognize the universality of the challenges faced by mothers. Frustrations, failures, fears, and flaws – these are common threads that weave through the tapestry of motherhood. The struggles our children face are struggles we've already faced. To become the mothers they need, we must be willing to evolve. If it requires mothering differently from that received from our own mothers, then so be it. Our children need our guidance to navigate their successful future.

The perpetuating cycle of conflict between parent and child continues unabated, an unyielding deadlock where neither side is willing to concede. Pride often prevails, with both asserting their righteousness. The mother asserting her authority and the child fervently arguing for their rights. Disrespect coincides with abuse, and the cycle seems unbreakable. Who will summon the courage to bring an end to this enduring tale? The origins of this cycle are elusive, lost in the mists of time, and the conclusion remains elusive. Generation after generation, the narrative persists.

THE CONQUEST

Observing others who shared the scars of emotional abuse, I noticed a pattern. Some, in a desperate bid to defy the odds manifested themselves as boisterous and aggressive, a shield against potential criticism that could shatter their fragile hearts. Those scarred by emotional abuse sought refuge in extremes, desperate to carve a niche for themselves where acceptance seemed elusive.

In the labyrinth of my struggles, a co-worker stood out as an emblem of resilience. Her responses to life's challenges left me in awe, prompting an unofficial interview. This co- worker's resilience became, for me, a beacon of possibility. Her ability to navigate life's challenges with grace and resilience became a source of inspiration and a catalyst for introspection.

Puzzled by the disparity in our responses, further conversations unveiled to me the role of personality types and love languages as buffers against the pain of emotional abuse. These diversities in personality types and love languages highlighted the nuanced ways individuals cope with emotional wounds. Understanding these differences became key to unlocking paths to healing.

The beast, emotional abuse, can be conquered through an arsenal of prayer, counselling, self-love, and determination, along with the scaffolding of support. Conquering the beast becomes a collective endeavour. The amalgamation of diverse strategies creates a formidable defense, gradually stripping away its power. Its bite, deadly and venomous, loses its potency when we refuse to be held captive any longer.

Again, through prayer, counselling, self-love, and unwavering determination, we can stand united against the relentless assault of emotional abuse.

Parents, it's time to pause and reflect. Draw from the wealth of experiences as children on the other side of the cycle. Pose these critical questions to yourself:

- Why am I so upset?

- What do I hope to achieve from this confrontation?

- Can I communicate firmly without resorting to disrespect?

Remember I chose to interpret my mother's actions as hatred. Little did I understand that her expressions of love were often clouded by fear, leading to frustration and confusion. I did not know then that her attempts to shield me from the pain and disappointment that she had endured remained unseen, buried beneath the weight of her *own* agony. I have learnt that confronting self-doubt is no small feat so I cannot judge her. The enemy of my soul had successfully sown doubt in my heart about who I was and what I was capable of. The journey out of emotional abuse involved dismantling the narrative that I was entitled to justice and love, without understanding the complexities of the fallen world.

As the layers of past experiences unraveled, the journey led to painful truths about the impact of my upbringing on my mothering style. Forgiveness, therefore, became an essential part of the process – a challenging act involving mercy and release, not so much of my own mother but, perhaps more difficult, towards myself. This act of forgiveness paved the way for healthier expressions of love for my own children and began the process of my healing

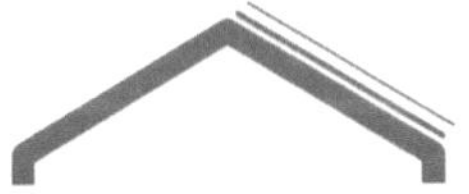

EXPERIENCING AND EXPRESSING HEALING GRACE

We, the wounded and scarred, stand in need of healing. For some, this journey may demand professional help, while for others, a conversation with a trusted friend, prayer, and introspection may suffice. Through recognition and seeking help, the path to healing unfolds. Healing is a journey of showing respect to ourselves and others, valuing both our worth and theirs. The antidote lies in treating ourselves with love and extending that grace to those around us. Love as the healing balm, soothes the wounds inflicted by emotional abuse.

By cultivating self-respect and extending the same courtesy to others, we dismantle the foundation on which the beast thrives. However, it is crucial that as we heal, we create a space for ourselves and others to make mistakes, embrace gratitude, and recognize small beginnings. These will help to minimise the possible return of the beast. In the effort to end the beast's bite, we will find healing and reclaim the beauty that was once stolen from us. Embracing our imperfections becomes a transformative act as we allow ourselves to grow. By fostering such an environment and acknowledging the journey's humble beginnings, we truly are breaking free from the chains that once bound us.

One of the most challenging aspects of my journey was revisiting painful experiences buried deep within. It required a level of introspection that, at times, felt overwhelming. There were moments when I questioned whether this journey was worth the emotional turmoil it stirred. However, with each revelation, I gained a clearer understanding of the root causes of my reactions.

The process of forgiveness, while difficult, also proved to be a cornerstone in my healing journey. Letting go of the pain associated with past experiences allowed me to embrace a new paradigm of love and understanding. It was a conscious decision to break free from the chains of resentment and to choose a path of compassion.

Now, those who have chosen this path of compassion for themselves will begin to experience God's healing grace. It then compels them to express this same healing grace to others, including their own children. For such parents, it becomes less difficult to see an unruly child or teenager as someone struggling to express themselves or grappling with a challenging day. Admittedly, achieving this perspective is an ongoing process, especially when patience is thin and immediate results are demanded. The desire for compliance, inherent in parenting, often clashes with the virtues of patience, persistence, and determination. But these clashes are the external manifestations of the inner workings of our emotional immune system.

Parents with a weak emotional immune system are often conditioned to seek rapid outcomes and sometimes unleash shouts and harsh words in a misguided effort to expedite change. However, understanding that impatience can lead to utterances that might not reflect true intentions underscores the importance of managing emotions and separating them from decision-making. This is the boost our emotional immune system needs. When the impulse to react immediately arises, consider taking a moment for deep breathing or a brief pause.

Healing is also expressed in trusting in God's plan for our children, allowing them to navigate their own experiences. This fosters growth. Rather than shielding them from life's challenges, focus instead on providing support and preparing to be a pillar of strength when they seek your guidance. Allowing our children to embrace the growth that arises from experiences, whether positive or challenging, becomes a crucial part of their journey.

Having experienced God's healing grace, we often also find ourselves compelled to express this healing to our abusive parents, but this is often the most difficult of all. I, therefore, encourage my friends struggling in this area to shift perspective and allow themselves to see their mothers' hearts crying out for them to become better versions of themselves. Amidst the hurt, I challenge all of us to uncover the positives and discern the good, even within the bad said or done. It may also help to envision our mothers in the labour room, pushing through the excruciating, inexplicable pain of birthing. Even if nothing else consoles you, it might bring solace to recognize that for many, our conception may have been merely a result of our parents' pleasure, and for others , our parents may have never truly desired us. However, there is solace in knowing that God not only wants us but meticulously planned every detail of our birth. As He said, "Before I shaped you in the womb, I knew all about you." (*Jeremiah 1:5a*). and as the psalmist declares, "Oh yes, you shaped me first inside, then out; you formed me in my mother's womb." (*Psalm 139:13*).

As I conclude, I reflect that it was amidst the confusion that the touch of Jesus became the catalyst for change. Recognizing my brokenness, I sought redemption and forgiveness. This touch impacted my actions on my children and fueled my determination to break the cycle of destructive parenting. It marked the beginning of my healing and of another journey, my road from victim to victory.

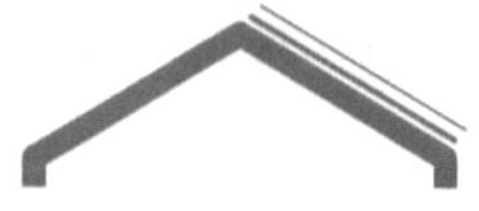

FROM VICTIM TO VICTOR

Reflecting on the analogy of a $5,000 bill hidden away, I grasped the significance of positioning. Placing oneself in the right position and timing enhances individual worth and relevance. In the journey of guiding, grooming, giving, and governing our children, we mentor them into purposeful lives. Recognizing their value allows them to pour out their unique contributions, making them not only useful but impactful.

According to the Oxford Dictionary, value is defined as "the regard that something is held to deserve; the importance, worth, or usefulness of something." While this definition should seamlessly apply to our own selves, many struggle to recognize their own value. This may stem from distorted self-images painted by external influences, comparisons to others, seeing oneself through the lens of external perceptions, or even a reluctance to introspect. To truly appreciate one's value requires a careful examination and, at times, deep self-reflection. It necessitates interest and a willingness to recognize the intricate qualities that contribute to one's worth.

Value becomes evident when there is a purpose. Even with diminished self-perception, one is still valuable and therefore very useful to society. However, to accurately perceive oneself is to value oneself. To value oneself is to acknowledge and understand one's function, purpose, and the quality of work invested in one's creation. Just as products are sometimes devalued due to ignorance of their production processes, individuals can underestimate their worth when oblivious to the profound craftsmanship involved in their creation.

In the depth of my reflection the intricacy of my journey became clear. Positioned on a higher ground I retraced the complex map I had charted and saw my transformation from a victim to a victor. The path traversed has been marked by struggles and battles with self-worth and a metamorphosis fueled by the transformative power of love. My determination to parent differently will ultimately break me free from the chains of victimhood.

The tempestuous years of adolescence became the crucible where the seeds of hatred found fertile ground within me. Frustrated by a constant sense of belittlement and an acute feeling of misfit, my internal landscape became a battleground. The world, once a place of potential allies, turned into a mine field of enemy territory, and trust became an elusive virtue. Hatred, rather than a fleeting emotion, became a coping mechanism, a shield against the perceived threats of a harsh and unforgiving reality.

The victim mentality manifested itself in a litany of constant complaints and silent comparisons. Unwilling to confront my own fears and insecurities, I projected the blame onto others. The noise of self-doubt became a relentless companion, drowning any semblance of self-worth and making me a prisoner to my own created limitations.

The transformative shift from victimhood to victory began with a stark realization – the only person to blame was myself! Rather than continuing to externalize my struggles, I needed to invest time in knowing myself intimately. The fear of failure, jeers, and mockery that had held me captive needed to be confronted. It was time to take risks, set goals, and live beyond the shadow of fear.

The transition involved shedding the victim mentality. Complaints turned into courageous actions, and silent comparisons transformed into bold attempts to showcase my worth. The fight was no longer against external adversaries but against the self-imposed limitations that had held me back for far too long.

Hatred and anger gradually gave way to a profound realization – I craved more from life. Beyond the pursuit of material success, I desired fulfilment and purpose. The unwavering love of God became my source of affirmation, attention, appreciation, and affection, the four pillars of transformation. Having the identity as a cherished child of the King superseded the echoes of past inadequacies.

Understanding the roots of victimization within my family provided a crucial paradigm shift in parenting patterns. Recognizing that victors plan for adversity instead of complaining and whining, I became intentional about strategizing and prioritizing obstacles to fulfil a greater purpose. This revolution serves as a testament to the power of spending time with Jesus and embracing His love- Soli Deo gloria (Glory to God alone)!

THE NEW LIFE

In the midst of my transformation, a deeper spiritual awakening occurred. Having recommitted my life to Christ in 2009, verses about purpose and divine plans started resonating within me. However, the joy of purpose was short-lived as my focus shifted to my children. I had to confront the reality that I hadn't sought God's plans for their lives.

In 2014, God's wisdom revealed a critical shift – my vessel needed repair. I had to learn to guide my children according to His plans. The journey wasn't instantaneous, but it has been transformative. Today, I am a better mother than I was, continuously mending with the guidance of the ultimate owner of life.

Forgiveness played a crucial role in this process. Letting go of pain was challenging, but it was the key to unlocking a healthier relationship with my children. It is not easy to love a parent who never loved you, but it is not impossible. With faith and the love of Christ, I began a journey of healing that transformed my relationships and my approach to motherhood.

Understanding the inherent value within myself and my children required a shift in perspective. The biblical principle of giving thanks in all things resonated, emphasizing the importance of gratitude in recognizing blessings.

Acknowledging the rarity and relevance of oneself increases worth and significance. Children groomed with affection, appreciation, acceptance, and affirmation naturally recognize their value, contributing positively to society. This transformative journey from unaware parenting to purposeful guidance underscores the importance of these four pillars. Breaking free from societal expectations, embracing gratitude, and recognizing intrinsic values, creates a foundation for a purpose-driven and fulfilling parenting experience.

Moreover, the journey from victim to victor need not be a daunting struggle for our children. As parents, we possess the profound ability to lead them to the love of God from an early age, sparing them from the pitfalls of victimhood.

By fostering a mindset of planning, analysing, and strategizing, we equip them to overcome obstacles and fulfil their unique purposes in life. The echoes of self-doubt can be replaced with the affirming voice that declares, "You are not just a product of circumstances; you are a child of the King, destined for purpose and significance." Therefore, in times of adversity and when grappling with ingrained habits, the knowledge of being purposefully created by a benevolent God, destined for prosperity and a fulfilling life, becomes a powerful anchor. It's crucial to distinguish between the shortcomings of our parents and the divine plan charted by a higher wisdom. Despite human flaws, God's purpose for our prosperity remains intact.

Guiding, grooming, and governing children into God's purpose for their lives involves helping them recognize and fulfil their purpose. Placing them in positions aligned with their purpose enables them to realize and apply their inherent value appropriately, guided by a higher purpose. This can be achieved with what I call *The Four Pillars of Holistic Development*:

1. *Appreciation:* Acknowledging the efforts and strengths of my children, cherishing their uniqueness, and fostering their self-esteem became the cornerstone of their self- awareness.

2. *Acceptance:* Overcoming societal norms, I learned to accept my children wholly, understanding that they are divine gifts entrusted to my care. Acceptance paved the way for genuine

love.

3. **Affirmation:** Conquering self-doubt, I began affirming my children's efforts. Instead of magnifying mistakes, I highlighted lessons that could be extrapolated, nurturing a positive environment for growth.

4. **Affection:** Bonding through affection, whether a comforting touch, a kind word, a smile, or a warm hug, solidified the healthy boundaries of intimacy.Affection is the thread that binds acceptance, appreciation, and affirmation.

Let's therefore now go and parent with purpose!

APPLICATION

As we close this book and resume our lives the question lingers, how do we practically apply all we have learned? I, therefore, take this moment to share practical applications to guide us.

My advice may be summarized in this emphasis I must and will stress: parents make it a habit to pray for, with, and over your children consistently. As such, you ensure that you speak words of life and blessing into their lives, setting a powerful spiritual precedent that will impact future generations. I do believe that this act of spiritual authority is transformative and enduring.

In addition, there are a series of practical activities and steps that may be done over and over again to strengthen us on our journey of becoming better persons and even overcoming *emotional abuse*.

VALUING ME

The concept of *"Valuing Me"* emerged when I began questioning the origins of my insecurities. Why did I grant others' words such power over me? Why did I permit myself to be so deeply affected? These inquiries revealed painful truths I had long suppressed. However, facing these truths became imperative; I could no longer dwell in self-doubt and comparison. I realized the need to liberate myself from the constraints of my own limiting beliefs. Thus, I commenced a journey of self-discovery — identifying my genuine wants and needs. Crucially, I learned to prioritize my own well-being. It is my wish that you, too, can gracefully navigate through the barriers of your heart, embracing your inherent value and aspirations with full sincerity.

Valuing Me

- What makes you feel valued?

- Who makes you feel valued?

- How often do you feel valued?
    - ( ) rarely ( ) Sometimes

- ( ) frequently ( ) Always

- How do you feel when you are not valued?

- Do you value you?
    - ( ) Yes ( ) No

- Do you think you allow others to devalue you? Why/Why not?

VALUING MY CHILD

"Valuing My Child" aims to encourage parents to contemplate aspects related to their child. Through responding to these questions, you will be able to articulate unspoken or undiscovered thoughts about your children.

- What are some of the things your child enjoys doing?

- List at least 5 things you would consider your child to be good at.

- Can you list areas of your child's life that need improvement?

- What do you believe your child is meant to be?

- What are some things you perceive to be hindrances to your child's success?

- In what ways can you intervene to prevent these hindrances?

- What is your belief/understanding of parenting?

- What do you consider a healthy parent child relationship?

- Do you think you have a healthy parent-child relationship? Why or why not?

- Do you believe parents and their children should have a healthy relationship? Why or why not?

- What are ways that parents can create healthy parent-child relationships?

BUILDING A HEALTHY PARENT CHILD RELATIONSHIP

Building a healthy parent-child relationship is a desire for most parents, as it is essential for the well- being and development of both the parent and the child. To foster this, I share six principles from one of my training sessions entitled, 'Building A Healthy Parent Child Relationship'. These are:

- creating a safe environment
- fostering mutual respect
- spending quality time
- developing consistency
- facilitating effective communication
- setting ground rules.

Please note, that some activities assigned to each principle may overlap. You are also not compelled to read through all principles at once.

1. Create a safe environment!

Creating a safe emotional environment for children is crucial for their well-being and development. Here are some strategies to help achieve that:

i. ***Open Communication:*** Encourage your children to express their feelings openly without fear of judgment. Listen actively and empathetically to what they have to say. Schedule regular "check-in" times with your children where they can share their thoughts and feelings without interruption. For example, during dinner, you can ask each family member to talk about the best and worst parts of their day.

ii. ***Validate Feelings:*** Let your children know that it's okay to feel a range of emotions and that their feelings are valid. Avoid dismissing or trivializing

their emotions. When your children express an emotion, acknowledge it, and provide validation. For instance, if your child is upset because he/she didn't do well on a test, you might say, "It's okay to feel disappointed. Let's talk about what we can do differently next time."

iii. ***Set Boundaries:*** Establish clear and consistent boundaries that provide structure and security. Children thrive when they know what to expect and feel safe within those parameters.

Clearly outline rules and expectations for behaviours. For example, you may establish a bedtime routine that includes specific times for brushing teeth, reading, and lights out. Consistently enforcing these boundaries helps children feel secure and also helps parents to manage ill-emotions.

iv. ***Model Healthy Expression:*** Be a positive role model by demonstrating healthy ways to manage and express emotions. Children often learn by observing the behaviours of adults around them. Let say, you're feeling stressed, instead of raising your voice or getting angry, demonstrate healthy habits such as going for a walk to cool off. You may also explain to your children, in the opportune moment, why you're using these strategies and how they can do the same. Also try avoiding yelling, name-calling, or using aggressive language during conflicts. It is also a good practice to apologize and take responsibility for your mistakes, showing your children that it's okay to admit when they're wrong.

v. ***Encourage Problem-Solving Skills:*** Help your children develop problem-solving skills by encouraging them to brainstorm solutions to challenges they encounter. This fosters resilience and confidence. Therefore, when your children encounter a problem, resist the urge to immediately provide a solution. Instead, ask open- ended questions to help them brainstorm possible solutions. For example, if they are having a conflict with a friend, you could ask, "What do you think you could do to resolve this?" You may also offer praise and encouragement for their efforts, even if the solution doesn't work out perfectly.

vi. ***Foster a Supportive Environment:*** Surround your children with supportive relationships, whether it's with family, friends, or mentors. Knowing they have a network of people who care about them can boost their emotional well-being. Encourage your children to participate in activities where they can build positive relationships, such as team sports, clubs, or community events. Additionally, make an effort to maintain strong connections with extended family members who can offer support and guidance.

vii. ***Teach Healthy Emotional Management Skills***: Teach your children healthy emotional management skills such as deep breathing, mindfulness, or engaging in constructive ethical activities they can use when feeling stressed or overwhelmed. Doing deep breathing exercises together with your children when they feel anxious or frazzled, is also helpful. In addition, consider creating a calm-down corner or space where your children can go to relax and recharge when they need a break. //Finally, it also good practice to encourage hobbies or activities that promote mindfulness such as drawing, journaling, or listening to music.

viii. ***Create Rituals and Routines:*** Establishing rituals and routines can provide a sense of stability and predictability, which helps children feel secure. You may establish daily or weekly rituals such as Friday movie nights, Sunday games evening or bedtime stories. Consistent routines help children feel safe and assured.

ix. ***Encourage Self-Care:*** Teach your children the importance of self-care and help them develop

habits that promote physical, emotional, and mental well-being. These activities include journaling, exercising, or spending time with friends.

x. ***Be Patient and Understanding:*** Understand that building a safe emotional environment takes time and patience. Be patient with your children and yourself as you navigate challenges and setbacks together. In the cases where your children make a mistake or face a challenge, resist the urge to criticize or blame. Instead, offer support and guidance while emphasizing that setbacks are a normal part of life. Show them that you're there for them, no matter what.

By implementing these strategies, you can create a safe emotional environment where your children feel supported, valued, and free to explore and express themselves.

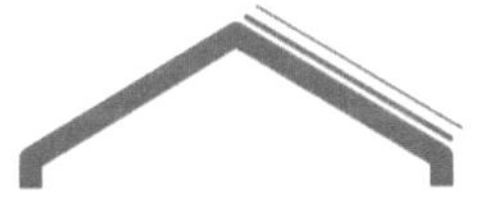

2. Facilitate mutual respect

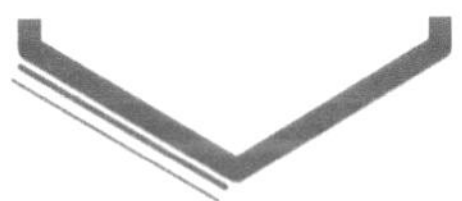

Facilitating mutual respect is crucial for building a healthy and positive parent-child relationship.

i. ***Model Respect:*** Children learn by observing their parents' behaviour. Treat your children with respect, kindness, and empathy. Show respect for their opinions, feelings, and boundaries. Example: when discussing family decisions, listen to their input attentively, even if it differs from your own. Say something like, "Ok. Let's consider it."

ii. ***Communicate Openly:*** Encourage open communication in your family. Listen to your children without interrupting, validate their feelings, and respond in a respectful manner. Create a safe environment where they feel comfortable expressing themselves. You may design family meetings, during which you can create a safe space for everyone to share their thoughts and feelings without judgment. Also, encourage your children to express themselves by saying, "We value your opinions, and we're here to listen. What would you like to share with us?"

iii. ***Set Clear Expectations:*** Establish clear rules and boundaries in your household. Involve your children in setting these rules and explain the reasons behind them. When expectations are clear, it helps to reduce conflicts and misunderstandings. Let's say you are establishing rules about screen time, it would be wise to involve your children in the decision making. Use the opportunity to explain why it's important to limit screen time. This fosters mutual understanding and respect for the rules.

iv. ***Encourage Independence:*** Allow your children to make age-appropriate decisions and take on reasonable responsibilities. It is also advised that you allow them age-appropriate autonomy as you support their efforts to become independent individuals. This could be activities such as setting the table, preparing a simple breakfast, packing their school bags or choosing their career path. Also, offer guidance when needed but allow them to complete tasks on their own. Acknowledge their efforts by saying, "I'm proud of how responsible you're becoming."

v. ***Teach Conflict Resolution:*** Teach your children healthy ways to resolve conflicts and disagreements. Additionally, encourage them to express their feelings assertively, listen to others' perspectives, and work towards finding a solution that respects everyone's needs. So, if siblings have a disagreement over sharing toys, guide them through a resolution process. Encourage them to listen to each other's perspective and brainstorm solutions together. Be sure to praise their efforts in finding a compromise, saying, "I'm impressed by how well you both communicated and found a solution."

vi. *Acknowledge Their Perspectives:* Recognize and validate your children's perspectives, even if you don't always agree with them. Show empathy and try to understand things from their point of view. For instance, if your child expresses frustration about a school assignment, validate their feelings

by saying, "I understand that you're feeling overwhelmed. Let's work together to break it down into smaller tasks." This shows empathy and respect for their emotions.

vii. **Avoid Negative Labels:** Refrain from using derogatory language or negative labels when addressing your children. Focus on the misbehaviour rather than making personal attacks. For example, instead of saying, "You're so lazy. You've not cleaned your room." Rather, focus on the behaviour by saying, "It's important to keep our room tidy. How do you think we can do that?" This avoids personal attacks and encourages problem-solving.

viii. **Praise Efforts and Achievements:** Celebrate your children's accomplishments and efforts, whether big or small. Encouragement and positive reinforcement help to build self-esteem and foster mutual respect. For example, if your children put effort into a project, acknowledge their hard work by saying, "I'm really impressed by the creativity and effort you put into this. You should be proud of yourself."

ix. **Apologize When Necessary:** Acknowledge your mistakes and apologize when you've acted disrespectfully or unfairly. This sets a powerful example. It shows that everyone makes mistakes and can take responsibility for their actions. Let's say you lose your temper and raise your voice during an argument. Afterwards you may say, "I'm sorry for raising my voice earlier. I was frustrated, but that wasn't the right way to handle it."

x. **Spend Quality Time Together:** Make time for meaningful interactions with your children. Engage in activities they enjoy. Also have conversations and create cherished memories together. You may capture the moment in a photograph or video. Building a strong connection strengthens mutual respect. Consider planning a family game night where everyone can bond and have fun together. Remember that fostering mutual respect is an ongoing process that requires patience, consistency, and empathy.

3. Spending quality time

Spending quality time with your children is essential for building strong bonds, fostering positive relationships, and creating lasting memories. It requires and emphasizes parents being present. Here are some tips on how to make the most of your time with your children:

i. ***Set aside dedicated time:*** Make a conscious effort to allocate specific time in your schedule for your children. This could be daily, weekly, or monthly depending on your availability. Schedule a weekly/monthly/quarterly/yearly "Family Fun Day" where you spend the entire day engaging in activities together, such as going to the zoo, having a picnic in the park, or baking cookies at home.

ii. ***Engage in activities they enjoy:*** Spend time doing things that your children love. Whether it's playing their favourite games, reading together, doing arts and crafts, or going for a walk in the park. Participating in activities they enjoy shows that you value their interests. An example for this activity could be a special "Craft Day" where you gather art supplies and spend the afternoon creating masterpieces together. Let your child choose the crafts and guide the activity. Be present!

iii. ***Be present:*** When you're spending time with your children, put away distractions like phones, laptops, or work-related thoughts. Give them your full attention and actively engage with them. This can be done by creating a "No-Tech Zone" where everyone puts their devices away and focuses on conversation during interactions. It also works best if you listen!

iv. *Listen actively:* Take the time to listen to your children's thoughts, feelings, and stories. Show genuine interest in what they have to say and ask open-ended questions to encourage conversation. Try to understand what is being said or done, before you respond.

v. *Create traditions and routines:* As mentioned before, establishing regular traditions or routines can provide a sense of stability and togetherness within your family. You can make these occasions extra special. Take movie nights, for instance, you may prepare popcorn, snuggle up with blankets and take turns in choosing movies.

vi. *Encourage open communication:* Create an environment where your children feel comfortable expressing themselves without fear of judgment. Encourage them to share their thoughts, concerns, and experiences with you. This can be achieved in family meetings where everyone has a chance to voice their opinions, suggest ideas, and discuss any issues. This creates a safe space where everyone's thoughts are respected.

vii. *Teach and learn together:* Use quality time as an opportunity for mutual learning and growth. Teach your children new skills or hobbies and be open to learning from them as well. In this case you can create a "Family Learning Day" where you pick a topic of interest and spend the day exploring it together. It could be anything from gardening to art & craft to learning a new language.

viii. ***Explore new experiences:*** Try out new activities and experiences together as a family. Whether it's visiting a museum, going on a nature hike, or trying a new sport, exploring new things together can be both fun and educational.

ix. ***Show affection and appreciation:*** Express your love and appreciation for your children regularly through hugs, kisses, and words of affirmation. Let them know how much they mean to you. You can choose to start a daily ritual of giving each family member a compliment (saying something you like about their physical attributes or clothes) or words of affirmation (such as an encouragement in doing something they are great at) during dinner. Also try to express gratitude for the little things they do and let them know how much you love them.

x. ***Be flexible and adaptable:*** Be open to spontaneous moments of connection and adjust your plans as needed to accommodate your children's interests and needs. From time to time, you will need to remain open to spontaneous adventures or changes in plans. If your child expresses interest in something unexpected, be willing to adjust your schedule to accommodate their interests and spend quality time together. Remember that quality time doesn't necessarily have to be extravagant or expensive. What matters most is love expressed in attention and the genuine connection you share with your children during the time you spend together.

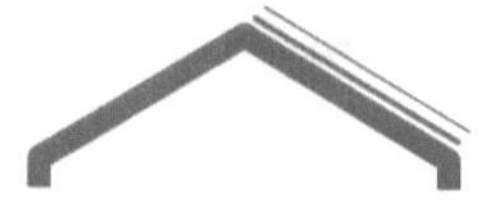

4. Developing consistency

Developing consistency with child/ren is essential for establishing routines, boundaries, and expectations. Here are some tips to help you achieve consistency:

i. ***Establish Clear Expectations:*** Clearly communicate your expectations to your children. Make sure they understand what behaviour is acceptable and what isn't. Again, I must reiterate, sit down with your children and discuss the household rules. For example, explain that everyone needs to clean up their toys after playing, and if they don't, there will be consequences like losing screen time.

ii. ***Be Firm but Fair:*** Stick to your rules and consequences consistently, but also be fair and reasonable, i.e. avoid being overly harsh or lenient. Let's take for example, if your children break the rule, the consequences must be enforced. Stick to these consequences each time a rule is broken, but also remember to be understanding if there is a genuine struggle. In this case, we offer support.

iii. ***Set Regular Routines:*** Create daily routines for activities like mealtimes, bedtime, homework, and chores. Consistent routines provide structure and predictability for children. A practical way to demonstrate this is by creating a visual schedule outlining daily routines and posting it in a common area of the house. Include times for waking up, meals, homework, playtime, and bedtime. Stick to this schedule as closely as possible to provide a sense of predictability for your children.

iv. ***Communicate Openly:*** Encourage open communication with your children. If there are changes to routines or rules, explain them clearly and listen to any concerns or questions your children may have. Thus, before implementing a new rule or making changes to routines, hold a family meeting to discuss the reasons behind your decision. Allow your children to express their thoughts and concerns and address them openly. For example, if bedtime is being pushed back by 30 minutes, explain why this change is necessary and listen to any worries they may have about it.

v. ***Be Patient:*** Consistency takes time and effort. Be patient with yourself and your children as you work together to establish consistent routines and behaviours. Understand that it may take time for your children to adjust to new routines and rules. As a result, you can stay consistent and patient, offering gentle reminders and encouragement along the way. Recognize and celebrate small successes to keep motivation high.

vi. ***Work as a Team:*** If you co-parent, make sure both you and the other parent are on the same page when it comes to rules and consequences. Consistency is more effective when all caregivers are aligned.

vii. ***Adapt as Needed:*** While consistency is important, it's also essential to be flexible and adapt to your children's changing needs. Review and adjust routines and rules as necessary.

Therefore, it may require you to periodically review the effectiveness of your routines and rules. If the needs of your children change or if something isn't working, be willing to adjust accordingly. For example, if your child is struggling with a particular rule such as bedtime, collaborate with them to find a solution that works better for everyone.

5. Fostering effective communication

Fostering effective communication with your children is essential for building strong relationships and understanding between you and them. Here are some tips to help you achieve that:

i. ***Create a Safe and Supportive Environment:*** Make sure your children feel safe and comfortable expressing themselves without fear of judgment or punishment. Let them know that you are there to listen and stand with them no matter what.

ii. ***Active Listening:*** Practice active listening by giving your full attention when your children are speaking. Maintain eye contact, nod, and provide verbal cues like "I see" or "I understand" to show that you are engaged and attentive.

iii. ***Encourage Openness:*** Encourage your children to share their thoughts, feelings, and concerns openly with you. Let them know that their opinions matter and that you are interested in hearing what they have to say.

iv. ***Be Empathetic:*** Show empathy and understanding towards your children's feelings and experiences. Validate their emotions and let them know that it's okay to feel the way they do. If your child is upset about something, empathize with them by saying things like, "I can see why you're feeling that way" or "It sounds like you're really frustrated." Let them know that it's okay to feel what they do and that you're there to empathize with them.

v. *Use Positive Reinforcement:* Acknowledge and praise your children for their efforts in communicating effectively. Positive reinforcement can help build their confidence and encourage them to continue sharing with you. When your children communicate effectively, whether it's expressing their feelings or articulating their needs, you can praise them by saying something like, "I'm proud of you for sharing that with me" or "You did a great job explaining how you feel."

vi. *Set Aside Quality Time:* Dedicate regular one-on- one time with each of your children to bond and communicate. This could be during mealtimes, bedtime, or special outings where you can have meaningful conversations without distractions. Schedule regular outings or activities with your child or with each child, to create opportunities for deeper conversations and strengthen your bond.

vii. *Be Patient:* Sometimes, children may find it difficult to express themselves or may take time to open up. Be patient and give them the time and space they need to feel comfortable sharing with you. If your child is hesitant to open up, don't try to force them to talk. Instead, let them know that you're available whenever they're ready and reassure them that you're there to listen whenever they need you.

viii. *Lead by Example:* Model good communication skills by being open, honest, and respectful in your own interactions with your children and others. Children often learn by observing the behaviour of adults around them. You can demonstrate healthy communication habits in your interactions with your child and others. For example, if you have a disagreement with your partner, model effective conflict resolution by calmly discussing the issue and finding a solution together.

ix. *Address Issues Promptly*: If there are any conflicts or issues that arise, address them promptly and constructively. Encourage your children to express themselves calmly and respectfully and also work together to find mutually agreeable solutions. If there's a conflict between siblings, facilitate a calm and respectful conversation where each child has a chance to express their perspective. Guide them in finding a compromise or solution that works for everyone involved.

x. *Seek Professional Help if Needed:* If you notice persistent communication challenges or underlying issues, consider seeking guidance from a family therapist or counsellor who can provide support and strategies tailored to your family's needs.

6. Setting ground rules

Setting ground rules for children is essential for maintaining structure, discipline, and harmony within the household. Here's a general guide on how to set ground rules effectively:

i. ***Involve Your Children:*** When setting ground rules, involve your children in the process. This helps them understand the reasons behind the rules and encourages their cooperation. Depending on their age, you can discuss what rules are necessary and why. Sit down with your children and discuss the household rules together. For example, if you're establishing a rule about screen time limits, ask your children how much screen time they think is reasonable and why.

ii. ***Keep it Simple and Clear:*** Ground rules should be easy to understand and remember. Avoid creating too many rules, as this can be overwhelming. Focus on the most important ones that are necessary for safety, respect, and maintaining order in the household. Think of creating a list of 3-5 fundamental rules that cover important aspects of behaviour, such as respecting others, completing chores, and following safety procedures. Post these rules in a visible place, like the kitchen or living room.

iii. ***Be Consistent:*** Consistency is key to enforcing rules effectively. Ensure that the rules apply to everyone in the household, including parents, and that consequences for breaking the rules are consistently enforced. If one of the rules is that toys must be put away before bedtime, make sure this rule is enforced every night. If toys are left out, gently remind your child to put them away and implement the previously stated consequence(s) if necessary.

iv. ***Set Age-Appropriate Rules:*** Consider the age and maturity level of your children when setting rules. Younger children may need simpler rules, while older children can handle more complex expectations. Adjust rules as your children grow and their needs change. For younger children, you might have a rule about holding an adult's hand while crossing the street, while for older children, you might have a rule about completing homework before playing video games.

v. ***Explain the Reasons Behind the Rules***: Help your children understand why certain rules are in place. This encourages them to see the purpose behind the rules and increases their likelihood of following them willingly. When establishing a rule about bedtime, explain to your children that sleep is important for their health and helps them feel energized and ready to learn the next day.

vi. ***Model Behaviour:*** Children learn by example, so it's important for parents to model the behaviour they want to see in their children. Follow the same rules you expect your children to follow by demonstrating respect, responsibility, and kindness in your interactions. If one of these rules is to speak respectfully to each other, make sure that both you and your partner model respectful communication in your interactions. Avoid yelling or using disrespectful language, even when you're frustrated.

vii. ***Encourage Open Communication:*** Maintain open lines of communication with your children so they feel comfortable discussing the rules, asking questions, and expressing concerns. This helps build trust and reinforces a sense of mutual respect within the family. Have regular family meetings where you discuss the household rules, address any concerns or questions your children have, and brainstorm solutions together if any rules are causing friction.

viii. ***Celebrate Successes:*** Acknowledge and celebrate when your children follow the rules and demonstrate positive behaviour. Positive reinforcement can motivate them to continue making good choices. For example, if your child consistently remembers to put their dirty clothes in the laundry basket, acknowledge their effort and perhaps even reward them with a small treat or extra playtime.

By following these steps, I believe you can establish clear and effective ground rules that promote a positive and harmonious family environment.

The journey continues.

ADDITIONAL RESOURCES

Below are the resources that have been invaluable on my journey to healing and redemption.

⬦ **Focus on the Family Broadcast** from *FOCUS ON THE FAMILY.COM* with host and cohost John Fuller Jim Daly

⬦ **Love Languages Quiz** from *5 LOVE LANGUAGE .COM* along with other materials from author Dr. Gary Chapman

⬦ **Love Style Quiz** from *HOW WE LOVE. COM* by author Milan & Kay Yerkovich

About the Author

Ms. Nathlee Grant has spent nearly 30 years in community development and in recent time focused particularly on developing and maintaining healthy parent-child relationships. She has launched numerous initiatives in this regard which never took off as expected, but boasted successes, nonetheless.

These include formal sessions such

as 'Youth and Adults Time 2 Talk', 'Teens Wise Up and Rise' and 'Who Am I'. Informally, Nathlee has advised many parents and even assisted in strengthening, encouraging and preserving their parent-child relationship.

In this newfound zeal of hers Ms. Grant has entered the whole new world of education completing her Post Graduate Diploma in Education and Training, graduating as valedictorian in 2022, and pursuing another Post Graduate Diploma in Learning Technologies simultaneously with a Master of Science Degree in Education and Leadership.

Moreover, Ms. Grant has interacted and built rapport with teens from many varied backgrounds through academic assistance. Furthermore, Ms. Grant has contributed to her son's school by advising frustrated parents, teachers and students and has remained among the best known and loved parents in his age group. She also stands respected in her family as a fountain of wisdom and a pioneer of change.

This book, years in the making, serves as her testament to the power of God and the power of change that can be made evident in every household, if every parent will allow it. If God changed an angry, emotionally abusive teenage mom, He can change you too!

www.ingramcontent.com/pod-product-compliance
Lightning Source LLC
Chambersburg PA
CBHW021139130726
47988CB00003B/1382